Herhood

Letters to Every Woman

Muzzafar Badder

Herhood: Letters to Every Woman

Published by – Self Published

"Every woman carries a story the world will never fully know; but those stories, in their quiet strength and unspoken sacrifices, are what hold this world together."

- **Muzzafar Badder**

//

To every Woman

To my Friends

To my Family

To the Humans

To the World

//

Herhood: Letters to Every Woman

Chapters:

Chapter 1: Dear Little Girls

Dear Little Girls,

You may not know it yet, but you are magic. The sparkle in your eyes, the way you ask endless questions about the world, the way you chase butterflies and build castles out of nothing but imagination; these are the first beautiful notes in the song of your life.

In your world, everything is a wonder. A flower blooming, a bird singing, the sky changing colors at sunset. You believe in fairies, heroes, and dreams that touch the clouds. And though you're small, your heart holds more courage than you realize.

But there will be moments when the world begins to change around you. When rules you never noticed before start to appear. You'll hear people tell you to sit properly, to speak softly, to behave like a "good girl." You might be asked to give up games you love because they're "not meant for girls." These words may seem small, but they carry a weight that can follow you for years.

You'll see how boys are allowed to be loud, to climb higher, to run faster without anyone asking them to stop. And you might wonder why you're asked to be careful while they are told to be brave. These things will confuse you. And they should.

But even in those moments, you'll show a kind of courage that most won't notice. Every time you stand up for yourself, every time you ask 'why not,' every time you laugh too loudly in a place where you were expected to stay quiet; you are already learning to be brave in a world that will expect you to be small.

You might not call it sacrifice yet, but in little ways, you will give up parts of yourself to fit in. You'll silence a question, you'll give up a dream, and you'll stay seated when you wanted to run. These moments will pass, but the strength you build by enduring them will stay with you.

One day, you'll look back and realize that you were always stronger than you were told. That your laughter mattered. That your stubbornness was a kind of wisdom. That your wild heart was never a flaw, but a gift.

So, dear little girls, hold on to your wonder. Keep dreaming of castles, keep believing in magic, and never let anyone convince you that your voice is too loud or your dreams too big. This world was built on the hopes of girls like you.

Thank you for your endless laughter, for your fearless hearts, and for the light you carry so effortlessly. Thank you for reminding us what it means to believe without fear. Keep shining. The world needs you.

With all my heart,
The Writer Who Sees You

Chapter 2: Dear Teenage Girls

Dear Teenage Girls,

This is a letter for the ones standing at the delicate edge between childhood and womanhood. For the hearts caught in between dreams and doubts, between wanting to grow up and wishing to stay small. I see you. I see the questions you carry, the fears you hide behind practiced smiles, and the moments when your heart feels far too heavy for your age.

You are at a stage where the world begins to notice you differently. Where compliments sometimes feel like burdens, and expectations come dressed as advice. People will start telling you who you should be, what you should wear, how you should speak, and what you should believe. They'll hand you invisible rules that don't always make sense. One day, you'll be told to be bold. The next, to be quiet. You'll be encouraged to dream, but only within limits they've set for you.

This is when you start learning about the world's double standards. How confidence in a boy is seen as leadership, while in you it might be called arrogance. How freedom granted to others comes to you with conditions. You'll see how opinions you once shared so freely are now questioned, doubted, or dismissed.

And through all this, you'll carry silent struggles. The ones you don't speak of; feeling too much, or not enough. Trying to be strong when you want to fall apart. Comparing yourself to faces in magazines, to friends who seem braver, louder, prettier, or more certain than you. You'll battle insecurities that no one notices. And still, you'll show up, every day, with a resilience you rarely get praised for.

You will sacrifice parts of yourself to belong. You'll trade honesty for acceptance. You'll silence your voice so someone else can feel louder.

You'll let go of dreams to avoid disappointing those you love. And while it might hurt, these moments will also shape you into someone unbreakable.

But let me remind you of this; you are allowed to be unsure. You are allowed to fall, to cry, and to feel lost. Growing up is not a race, and strength does not mean being unshaken all the time. There is courage in vulnerability. There is power in admitting, "I don't know."

Keep asking your questions. Keep chasing the dreams they told you to leave behind. Laugh too loud. Stand too tall. Love yourself when it feels hardest. Because this world has tried to quiet girls like you for generations, and every time you speak your mind or choose your own path, you are breaking chains for those who will come after you.

Thank you for your bravery in navigating a world that often forgets how heavy teenage years can be. Thank you for your restless hearts, your stubborn hope, and your silent strength. You are far more extraordinary than you realize.

With all my heart,
The Writer Who Sees You

Chapter 3: Dear Sisters

Dear Sisters,

This is for every girl who has grown up sharing rooms, secrets, clothes, and sometimes silent rivalries. For those bound not just by blood, but by years of shared glances, unspoken understandings, and the kind of love that survives both laughter and loud arguments.

Being a sister is its own kind of story. It's a bond that starts in childhood and stretches quietly across years, even when life tries to pull you apart. I see the way you learn to be both a friend and a rival, a protector and a critic. I see the way you carry each other's burdens without always knowing how to say it out loud.

But being a sister also comes with a weight you don't always speak of. Especially in homes where there's a brother; older or younger; the expectations are different. You learn early on to give up things for the sake of peace. You stay home while he goes out. You're asked to compromise, to adjust, to understand that "he's a boy, things are different for him." You watch freedoms being handed out unequally, and though it stings, you learn to swallow it.

You sacrifice small things at first; turns to speak, chances to play, dreams you quietly fold away. Later, you sacrifice your opinions at the dinner table, your choices in family decisions, and sometimes, your own dreams because "it isn't what's expected." You see how your role is to nurture, to mend, to quietly hold the pieces together, while he's allowed to be reckless, bold, and unapologetic.

And still, you carry love in your heart. You protect him, even from his own mistakes. You defend him when others won't. You carry his secrets, share his burdens, and when needed, you stay up waiting, worrying, praying in silence. You become a shield and a shelter, often without a word of recognition.

There are days when you ache under this unseen weight, when the unfairness sits heavy in your chest. But you rise, you smile, you make space. Because that's what you've been taught to do. Because that's what sisters have done for generations.

As you grow, you might drift apart. Distance comes, new priorities arrive, and sometimes, you lose touch with the girl who once knew everything about you. Life has a way of scattering people, but the thread between sisters holds, even when stretched thin. And through it all, you still carry the stories, the wounds, and the wisdom that comes from being the girl who learned to survive in the spaces between.

Thank you, sisters, for your silent sacrifices. For the times you put your dreams on hold, for the words you never said, for the peace you kept, even when you longed to scream. Thank you for the fights that taught forgiveness and the laughter that healed wounds no one else could. You are the quiet backbone of so many homes, the keeper of stories, the first friend many of us ever had, and often the one who carries the weight of family expectations with grace.

Even if you've grown apart, even if words are scarce now, know this; you matter. You are loved. You are irreplaceable.

With all my heart,
The Writer Who Sees You

Chapter 4: Dear Daughters

Dear Daughters,

This letter is for you; the ones who fill homes with laughter, tenderness, and a love so deep it often remains unspoken. I see you. I see the light you bring into a family, the warmth you carry in your heart, and the sacrifices you quietly make, not because anyone asked you to, but because you love too deeply to let your parents carry their burdens alone.

From the moment you entered this world, you became a part of someone's story; a daughter, a joy, a responsibility, and often, an unspoken hope. As you grew, your love for your parents grew too. You learned to read the lines on your mother's face, the worry in your father's eyes, the heaviness in their hearts; and you carried pieces of it as your own.

You gave up small things at first; a toy you loved because it was too expensive, a trip you wanted to take because the family needed to save, dreams you quietly folded away because you didn't want to be a burden. And later, those sacrifices grew. You made choices based on what your parents wanted for you. You stayed home when your heart longed to explore. You accepted decisions you didn't agree with because you didn't want to disappoint them.

There is a love daughters carry that words can't hold. It's in the way you check if your mother has eaten, in the way you notice your father's tired eyes, in the way you defend them when others don't understand. It's in your silence during arguments, in the way you choose peace over pride, in the way you lower your voice even when your heart is screaming.

And sometimes, you carry wounds too. The moments when you felt less valued, when your opinions were dismissed, when your sacrifices went unnoticed because "this is what good daughters do." You learned to accept less than you deserved, to settle, to adjust; all for the sake of your family's happiness.

But let me tell you this: your love is extraordinary. The world might not see it, and your parents might not always express it, but it lives in every quiet prayer they whisper for you, in every proud look they try to hide, in every small thing they do to protect you, even if they don't know how to say it out loud.

Thank you, daughters, for being gentle hearts in a world that can be unkind. For your silent sacrifices, your fierce loyalty, your unshakable love. Thank you for carrying your family's hopes and wounds with grace. You are not just someone's daughter; you are the quiet courage of every home.

With all my heart,
The Writer Who Sees You

Chapter 5: Dear Housewives

Dear Housewives,

This is a letter for the women who left their own homes behind to build someone else's. For those who stepped into unfamiliar walls, carrying old memories in their hearts and new responsibilities in their hands. I see you. I see the quiet strength it takes to leave behind the comfort of your parents' house, to say goodbye to the nameplate that felt like home, and to enter a world where you were expected to adjust before you could even understand your place in it.

They promised you many things, didn't they? Sweet words, hopeful dreams, a life where you would be cherished. And maybe some of those promises were kept. But many were quietly forgotten, lost in the busyness of life, in the demands of tradition, in the quiet assumptions made about what a wife should do, should be, and should endure.

You became the one who woke up earlier and slept later. The one who learned recipes you never liked, traditions you never questioned, and rules that were never spoken out loud but were expected to be known. You gave up the way you liked your tea, the songs you listened to in the morning, the clothes you loved to wear; all for the sake of acceptance, for the fear of being called difficult.

And then came the sacrifices no one saw.

You put your own dreams on hold so his could rise. You smiled on days you wanted to cry because you knew your tears would be called weakness. You let go of hobbies, friendships, parts of yourself, and sometimes even your voice, just to keep the peace in a house that wasn't built for you but now rested on your shoulders.

You tried to win hearts. To impress people who measured your worth not by the kindness of your heart, but by the softness of your tone, the taste of your food, the obedience in your actions. You became a daughter-in-law, a wife, a caretaker, a host, a problem-solver; wearing a hundred different roles, often without a word of thanks.

And through it all, you stood strong.

You found joy in small victories; a smile from your mother-in-law, a quiet moment of kindness from your husband, a child's laughter, a peaceful evening after a long, restless day. You created a home out of walls that were never yours and built a life out of responsibilities you never asked for but carried with grace.

Thank you for your patience, for the endless efforts you pour into others while your own heart sometimes runs empty. Thank you for being the silent strength behind families, the one who remembers everyone's birthdays, favorite dishes, and quiet needs. Thank you for the sacrifices that no one talks about; the ones that shaped homes, nurtured families, and held generations together.

Even when your name fades behind titles like wife, mother, or daughter-in-law; you remain extraordinary.

With all my heart,
The Writer Who Sees You

Chapter 6: Dear Mothers

Dear Mothers,

This letter is for you; the woman, who does everything, feels everything, gives everything, and asks for nothing. I see you. I see the hands that hold, the heart that worries, the eyes that search, and the soul that never truly rests.

You carry the weight of so many lives in your hands. From the moment you become a mother, you stop belonging entirely to yourself. Every heartbeat, every decision, every dream is quietly measured against what your children need, what your family requires, what your home demands. And even on the days when you feel like breaking, you hold it together, because that's what you believe a mother must do.

You wake before the sun, not for yourself, but for the ones you love. You prepare, you plan, you clean, you teach, you scold, you forgive, and you start again. You remember birthdays, favorite meals, medicines, appointments, school projects, and unspoken fears. You are the first to notice when something is wrong, and the last to ask for help when you need it.

And the world forgets, sometimes, that behind this title of 'Mother' stands a woman. A woman who once had dreams that had nothing to do with marriage or motherhood. A girl who laughed loudly, dreamed recklessly, and believed in a world built on possibilities. That girl still exists somewhere inside you; quietly watching from behind the responsibilities.

You made sacrifices that no one ever saw. You let go of friendships, career opportunities, hobbies, rest, and sometimes even your health. You gave up your favorite dress because a school fee was due. You stopped visiting places you loved because there was no one to watch the kids. You made peace with being taken for granted because you knew your family needed you more than it needed your complaints.

And yet; you love. Fiercely, protectively, endlessly.

You became a shield against the world's cruelty. You stood between your children and their heartbreak. You believed in them when they didn't believe in themselves. You loved them through their mistakes, their rebellions, their ungrateful days. You whispered prayers over their sleeping heads, wiped their tears, and stitched their world back together when it fell apart.

Thank you, Mothers, for the days you stayed strong when you were breaking. For the smiles you faked so your children could stay brave. For the meals you made without appetite. For the nights you stayed awake worrying about problems you could never share.

You are the silent strength of every home. The heart of every family. The story behind every success. And though the world may forget to say it; you are everything.

With all my heart,
The **Son** Who Sees You

Chapter 7: Dear Working Women

Dear Working Women,

This letter is for you; the ones who rise before the sun, who lace their shoes, tie their hair, and step out into a world that so often questions your worth, your choices, and your strength. I see you, walking into offices, factories, classrooms, hospitals, markets, and boardrooms with a heart full of responsibilities no one else can fully comprehend.

You carry more than a bag or a briefcase. You carry expectations; of being good daughters, supportive wives, caring mothers, dutiful daughters-in-law, and dependable sisters. You carry guilt, too. The kind that creeps in when you miss a school function, when you leave a sick parent at home, when dinner isn't ready on time, when your own health is neglected because you've prioritized everyone else.

You've been asked to prove yourself in places where your voice was dismissed. You've been told to be tougher, to smile more, to not be "too ambitious." You've worked twice as hard to be considered half as capable. And while the world celebrates your achievements on posters and campaigns, it conveniently forgets to mention the days you went to work with a breaking heart, the evenings you came home to chores and duties while your own exhaustion was invisible.

You've sacrificed countless dreams, promotions, vacations, and sometimes even your mental peace; not because you lacked the ability, but because you placed family needs first. You've endured judgments for choosing to work, for earning more than your husband, for delaying marriage, for having children and continuing your job, or for not having children at all.

And in all of this, you've stayed strong. Not because you had no choice, but because you believed in creating a life on your own terms. You've built identities beyond surnames and relationship titles. You've inspired younger girls watching you from a distance, quietly learning how to dream a little bigger.

So today, I want to thank you; for every early morning, every late night, every moment you swallowed your pain and smiled anyway. For carrying both your world and theirs. For showing up, even when the world didn't make it easy. You are the heartbeat of progress, and your courage shapes generations.

This world may never fully repay what you've given it, but I hope you pause sometimes and feel proud of the battles you've fought and the life you've built. Because you, dear working woman, are remarkable.

With respect and gratitude,
The Writer Who Sees You

Chapter 8: Dear Unmarried Women

Dear Unmarried Women,

This letter is for you; the women who have heard the same questions again and again: *"When are you getting married?" "Don't you feel lonely?" "What's wrong?"* Society has built its own expectations around you, as though your worth is measured by a ring on your finger, a wedding in your photo album, or the surname you carry.

But I see you. And I see the quiet strength it takes to live life on your own terms in a world that expects you to follow a script.

Some of you chose this path; choosing freedom, self-discovery, peace, and independence over a relationship that didn't feel right. Some of you had other dreams, ambitions that asked for your attention, and you listened. Some of you stayed single because the one you loved left, or life simply didn't unfold the way you hoped it would. And some of you were told by fate, by loss, or by silence, that marriage wasn't meant to be part of your story; at least not yet.

And through it all, you've carried yourself with grace. You've faced awkward glances at family gatherings, endured careless jokes about being too choosy or too modern. You've watched friends post wedding pictures and baby announcements while you silently celebrated your own quiet victories; a promotion, a solo trip, a book you finally finished, a garden you nurtured, a life you built by yourself.

You've made sacrifices too. The ones no one talks about. The lonely dinners, the absence of someone waiting for you at home, the societal labels that cling to you like shadows. You've carried the weight of assumptions; that you must be sad, incomplete, or stubborn. And yet, you've lived.

You've cared for parents when there was no one else. You've filled your life with friendships, with dreams, with work, with travels, with books, with simple joys that belong to you alone. And in doing so, you've redefined what it means to be fulfilled, to be complete.

I want to thank you; for choosing yourself. For surviving in a society that romanticizes marriage but forgets that a woman's worth is not defined by a man's last name. For showing younger girls that happiness isn't a destination marked by a wedding date, but something you can find in the life you carve with your own hands.

Your courage is quiet, but it's powerful. And though the world might not always applaud you, I hope you wake up knowing that you are enough; exactly as you are.

With love and respect,
The Writer Who Sees You

Chapter 9: Dear Divorced Women

Dear Divorced Women,

This letter is for you; the women who once stood at the start of forever with hope in your hearts, believing in promises, building homes, and sharing names. You entered marriage the way most women do; with trust, compromise, and silent sacrifices. And when it all came undone, you stood at a crossroads the world never truly prepares women for.

I see the courage it took to say *enough.*
The world talks about love, but no one teaches you how to walk away from it when it turns into pain, silence, neglect, or indifference.
People forget how much strength it takes for a woman to leave behind what she built, knowing she'll be questioned, judged, labeled, and blamed.

Some called you selfish, some said you didn't try hard enough, and some whispered that you'd be alone forever. They pitied you at family functions, spoke about you in hushed voices, and asked you to stay quiet; to accept things, for the children, for your family, for society's approval.

But you chose yourself.
You chose peace over pretense.
You chose healing over pretending.
And for that, you are remarkable.

You've lived through the heartbreak of not just a relationship ending, but of dreams being shattered, of homes being divided, of friendships taking sides, and of your own reflection changing in the mirror.

You've held back tears when signing papers, packed memories in boxes, and faced nights when loneliness felt unbearable.

And yet, you survived.

You rebuilt yourself piece by piece; perhaps with a new job, a different city, a small room of your own, or by simply waking up each day and choosing to keep going.

Your sacrifices are invisible to the world; the birthdays you celebrated alone, the strength it took to raise your children single-handedly, or the sheer resilience of learning how to pay bills, fix appliances, and fight legal battles. You carried your pain with grace, and your silence spoke louder than a thousand words.

I want to thank you; for reminding the world that a woman's life doesn't end with a broken marriage. That divorce is not failure, but sometimes the most powerful declaration of self-worth.

You are not a label, not a rumor, not a cautionary tale.
You are a survivor.
You are a warrior.
And you are allowed to find love again, in others, in yourself, or in the life you choose to create from here.

With deepest respect and pride,
The Writer Who Sees You

Chapter 10: Dear Widows

Dear Widows,

This letter is for you; the women who loved, who built lives alongside someone, and who were left holding fragments of forever far too soon. No one prepares a woman for this kind of loss. The world celebrates brides, but seldom speaks of widows. And yet, you exist, carrying a grief so deep it becomes a language only your heart understands.

I see you.

I see the strength it takes to wake up in a home that feels emptier than it should, to face anniversaries and birthdays marked by absence. You've lived through nights where silence felt deafening, and mornings where you had to pretend to be strong for children, for families, for yourself.

You've been called brave when you didn't want to be. You've been expected to move on when you barely learned how to survive.
You've had to mourn not just the man you loved, but the life you planned, the dreams you shared, and the years you were promised.

Society, with its careless words, has tried to wrap you in labels; calling you unfortunate, pitiful, or in some cruel cases, a burden. They've expected you to shrink, to disappear, to live in the shadows of your loss, forgetting that you are still a woman with a heart, desires, and a right to joy.

And yet, you carried on.
You've wiped your own tears in empty rooms.
You've raised children with both hands; one holding them close, and one wiping away your grief.
You've stood through ceremonies, festivals, and gatherings, with a smile that concealed more sorrow than anyone will ever know.

Your sacrifices go unnoticed by many; the birthdays you quietly celebrated alone, the festivals you attended for the sake of family, the bravery it took to handle paperwork, financial struggles, loneliness, and unsolicited advice. But here's what I want you to know: **you are not forgotten.**

You are not a shadow of your past life. You are not a half-life. You are a full woman, one who has endured the kind of loss most hearts wouldn't survive. And you still wake up. You still live. That is nothing short of extraordinary.

I want to thank you; for carrying memories like sacred keepsakes, for loving so deeply, and for surviving so courageously. For proving that even in the face of unimaginable loss, a woman's spirit can endure, rebuild, and rise again.

You deserve softness, love, and light, now and forever.

With reverence and love,
The Writer Who Sees You

Chapter 11: Dear Grandmothers

Dear Grandmothers,

This letter is for you; the women who've lived through decades of changing seasons, carrying wisdom in your eyes and warmth in your arms. You are the storytellers, the silent protectors, the gentle hearts who've witnessed the world transform around you, yet held on to the simple, unshakable truths of life.

I see you; with your wrinkled hands that once carried infants and now hold generations. You've lived through times when your voice was seldom asked for but always needed. You've sacrificed silently, given endlessly, and taught without expecting anything in return.

You were the girls who were married too young, the women who raised families with little but made it seem like enough. You were the mothers who scolded and soothed, who cooked for a table full of children and then ate whatever remained at the end. You were the ones who stood behind your families like a backbone no one noticed until it bent with age.

And now, as a grandmother, you are the keeper of traditions and secrets, of lullabies and old remedies. You've watched your children grow, stumble, succeed, and you've watched your grandchildren arrive with their curious eyes and boundless energy; each one a piece of your heart reborn.

But it hasn't always been easy, has it?

You've endured the loneliness of empty homes after marriages, jobs, and new lives carried your loved ones elsewhere. You've carried grief when you lost old friends, or a spouse who once held your hand through life's battles. You've sometimes felt left behind in a world too fast, too loud, and too new.

And still, you remain; the quiet anchor. You've sacrificed personal dreams, the right to complain, and sometimes even your dignity for the sake of family peace. You've smiled through physical pains and emotional aches because you never wanted to burden anyone.

I want to thank you; for your sacrifices, both visible and unseen. For every bedtime story, every old recipe, every word of advice offered without demand. For being the soul of a home, even when you're not always asked. For loving fiercely in a world that often overlooks the elderly, forgetting that you were once the hands that shaped it.

You are more than a grandmother.
You are history, courage, tenderness, and wisdom in its most human form.

With love, honor, and endless gratitude,
The Writer Who Sees You

Chapter 12: Dear Single Mothers

Dear Single Mothers,

This letter is for you; the women who carry entire worlds on their shoulders. The ones who fill both roles at home: the hand that comforts and the voice that disciplines, the protector and the provider, the soft place to fall and the firm ground to stand on.

I see you; rising before dawn, packing lunches, managing homework, calming tears, fixing broken toys, and chasing after bills, jobs, and your own scattered pieces. You've become experts in pretending everything is fine while carrying silent storms inside. The world sees your smile, but rarely the weight behind it.

Some of you lost a partner to life's cruel turns. Some were abandoned. Some chose to walk away from relationships that became too heavy to bear. And some never had anyone to begin with. Yet in every story, there's one thing in common: you stayed. You fought. You loved.

You've sacrificed more than most people realize.
You've skipped meals so your child could eat.
You've worn the same clothes for years so they could have new books, better shoes, and brighter futures.
You've set aside your own dreams and desires because there was never enough time, money, or energy left for you.

And through it all, you've faced judgments and whispered assumptions. People questioned your decisions, your strength, your worth. Some treated you as though being a single mother was a flaw, when in truth, it's a badge of unmatched courage.

I want to thank you; for every sleepless night, every tear shed in secret, every birthday you made special with too little. For every illness you managed alone, every school event you attended with no one by your side, and every victory you quietly celebrated because no one else was there to notice.

You’ve taught your children resilience, loyalty, and the extraordinary strength of a mother’s love. You’ve proven that a woman doesn’t need a partner to build a family, to offer security, to raise good people. You’ve shown the world that love isn’t about numbers; it’s about presence, about sacrifice, about a heart that refuses to give up.

You are fierce, tender, flawed, and fearless. And while the world may overlook you, I hope you never overlook yourself.

Because you, dear single mother, are one of the bravest women walking this earth.

With endless respect and love,
The Writer Who Sees You

Chapter 13: Dear Women Who Couldn't Become Mothers

Dear Women Who Couldn't Become Mothers,

This letter is for you; the women who silently carry an ache the world rarely notices. The ones whose arms longed to hold, whose hearts had already made space for a child, but for reasons cruel or unexplained, never did.

I see you.

I see the way you've smiled through other people's baby showers, blessed newborns, and pretended it didn't hurt when someone casually asked, *"When are you having yours?"* I see the polite nods, the diverted eyes, and the quiet withdrawal from conversations that sting a little too sharply.

You've lived through the heaviness of doctor visits, hopeful prayers, endless treatments, or the emptiness of unanswered prayers. You've felt betrayed by your own body, or by fate, or by the unfairness of it all. Some of you tried for years, some knew from the start, and some held hope until it quietly left.

You've sacrificed dreams too.
The holidays you wished you'd spend with little hands tugging at your dress.
The lullabies you never sang.
The birthdays you imagined but never planned.

And still; you've continued.
You've poured your love into nieces, nephews, students, neighbors' children, friends' little ones, or fur babies. You've mothered in a thousand other ways; as a mentor, a sister, a confidante, a healer. Your nurturing heart didn't disappear; it just found different homes.

I want to thank you; for your courage, for your grace, for surviving a kind of loss that doesn't always have a name. For walking through life with a brave face while carrying invisible grief. For loving others' children when you couldn't have your own, and for finding joy where pain tried to plant itself.

You are not less.
You are not incomplete.
You are not defined by what your body did or didn't do.

You are a whole woman; fierce, nurturing, tender, and infinitely worthy of love and honor. Your existence matters, your story matters, and your heart is enough.

With softness, strength, and boundless respect,
The Writer Who Sees You

Chapter 14: Dear Pregnant Women

Dear Pregnant Women,

This letter is for you; the women carrying life within them, feeling tiny heartbeats beneath their own, and experiencing a miracle that words so often fall short of capturing. You are the bridge between two worlds: one you've known, and one that's about to begin.

I see you.

I see your glow, your swollen feet, your restless nights, your racing thoughts. I see the quiet fears you don't always voice; the worries about whether you'll be enough, whether you're doing everything right, whether your child will arrive safe, healthy, loved. I see the silent sacrifices already unfolding in your life.

From the moment you discovered those two lines on a test, you began a journey of giving. Giving your body, your peace, your comfort, your time, your sleep. Your cravings, your nausea, your aches, your hormonal storms; all part of this sacred, complicated, beautiful journey.

Some of you are carrying your first child, filled with nervous excitement. Some have known loss before and now cradle both hope and fear. Some carry alone, abandoned or unsupported. And some carry after years of waiting, tears, and prayers answered in their own time. Every story, every pregnancy, carries its own courage.

You've already made sacrifices.
Giving up certain foods, habits, routines. Enduring uncomfortable scans and tests, adjusting to a body that no longer belongs only to you.
You've faced judgment; too big, too small, too active, too fragile.
Endless advice, uninvited opinions, and the weight of expectations.

And still; you carry on.
You talk to the life inside you, sing to it, dream about its future. You endure discomfort with grace. You imagine the day you'll hold this little soul in your arms and forget every ache and sleepless night.

I want to thank you; for your strength, for your bravery, for loving a heart you've never seen, for enduring pain most will never witness. For creating life in a world that sometimes forgets the price women pay for it.

You are not just expecting a baby.
You are carrying generations.
You are birthing tomorrow's world.
And that, dear woman, is one of the greatest things anyone can do.

With tenderness, admiration, and love,
The Writer Who Sees You

Chapter 15: Dear New Mothers

Dear New Mothers,

This letter is for you; the women who have just stepped into the most sacred, beautiful, exhausting, and overwhelming chapter of their lives. You are holding tiny, fragile lives in your arms, while carrying the weight of endless responsibilities and emotions you never knew existed.

I see you.

I see the sleepless nights, the sore arms, the aching back. I see the tears you cry in the dark, sometimes from exhaustion, sometimes from joy, and often because no one warned you how heavy this love could feel. I see you looking down at your baby's face, wondering if you're doing this right, and fearing every little thing.

You've already made sacrifices.
You've given your body, your time, your sleep, and your independence. You've put your needs last without hesitation. Some of you are recovering from painful deliveries, C-sections, or the invisible wounds of labor. Some of you are navigating motherhood without the support you expected, feeling more alone than you imagined possible.

You've faced judgment for every choice; how you feed your baby, how you hold them, how soon you leave the house, whether you sleep when they sleep, whether you ask for help. The world will always have opinions about how you should mother. But listen closely, dear new mother: **there's no one right way. There's only your way.**

It's okay to feel overwhelmed.
It's okay to miss your old life.
It's okay to grieve parts of yourself while falling deeply in love with this tiny human.

You are allowed to be tired, frustrated, elated, and terrified; all at once. Because motherhood, especially in its earliest days, is a storm of contradictions: joy and fear, hope and exhaustion, love and loss of control.

I want to thank you; for giving your all when you feel you have nothing left. For holding your baby through tears, for learning to understand tiny cries, for surviving on little sleep and endless worry. For being a source of warmth, food, safety, and comfort, even when your own needs go unmet.

You are more than enough.
Even when you doubt yourself, even when the days blur together, even when no one says thank you; your presence is a miracle in your child's life.

And though you may not hear it often, you are doing an incredible job.
You are not alone.
And you are deeply, deeply loved.

With gentle love, admiration, and respect,
The Writer Who Sees You

Chapter 16: Dear Women in Abusive Relationships

Dear Women in Abusive Relationships,

This letter is for you; the women whose stories are often buried behind closed doors, whose bruises aren't always visible on the skin, and whose voices have been silenced by fear, shame, or hopelessness. I write this to tell you: **I see you. I believe you. And you matter.**

I see the way you've learned to measure the room by a glance, the way you weigh every word before speaking, the way you apologize for things that were never your fault. I see the courage it takes just to survive each day in a world where you feel trapped, isolated, or broken.

Your sacrifices go unnoticed by many.
You've stayed for the sake of children, for financial survival, for the fear of loneliness, or because somewhere in your heart you held onto hope that things might change. You've sacrificed your peace, your dignity, your freedom, and your dreams. You've shrunk yourself to fit into spaces where you were never meant to suffer.

And yet; here you are, still standing.
Still breathing.
Still hoping.
Even in the darkest corners of your life, you've protected your spirit, though battered and bruised. You've been blamed for your pain, made to believe you're the reason for the cruelty you endure. But let me remind you, with unwavering certainty: **it is never your fault.**

You are not weak.
You are not foolish.
You are not undeserving of love or safety.

What you are; is strong in ways most cannot comprehend. It takes unimaginable strength to live with fear and still care for your children, to smile in public, to hold yourself together when inside you're unraveling.

I want to thank you; for surviving in silence when you had no choice, for protecting others even when you couldn't protect yourself, for keeping your heart beating when everything around you tried to crush it. You've endured what no one ever should have to. And I pray you find the strength, the support, and the freedom to leave, to heal, and to rebuild your beautiful life in a world where no one has the right to harm you.

You deserve safety.
You deserve love without fear.
You deserve a life where you can breathe freely, laugh loudly, and be wholly yourself without apology.

And when you find that life, know that you are not starting over; you are finally coming home to yourself.

With boundless empathy, strength, and love,
The Writer Who Sees You

Chapter 17: Dear Brave Survivors

Dear Brave Survivors,

This letter is for you; the women who have endured the unthinkable and still found a way to breathe, to rise, and to exist in a world that once tried to break you. Whether your battles were against violence, abuse, illness, betrayal, heartbreak, or loss; you are a testament to the kind of courage that lives deep in a woman's bones.

I see you.

I see the strength it takes to get out of bed when your heart feels heavy. I see the bravery it takes to smile when your soul still carries scars. I see the quiet victories no one else notices; getting through a day without breaking, speaking up for yourself, trusting again, laughing for the first time in too long.

You've faced storms that others would drown in.
You've been betrayed by people who should have protected you.
You've lived through nights darker than most can imagine. And even though you sometimes feel damaged or different, I want to remind you: **you are not your pain. You are not what happened to you. You are what you've chosen to become after it.**

You've sacrificed pieces of your innocence, your trust, your sense of safety; all in the fight to survive. You've rebuilt yourself from ruins, carrying both your wounds and your wisdom. Some of those scars are still tender. Some you've learned to wear like armor.

I want to thank you; for your unshakable resilience. For every tear you wiped alone. For refusing to let your story end in defeat. For showing the world that survivors are not weak; they are warriors. For being a quiet, steady hope to other women who feel lost in their own battles.

Your survival matters.
Your voice matters.
Your story matters.

And though you might not feel it every day; you are loved, valued, and deeply admired. Not for what you went through, but for the woman you've become because of it.

This world needs you, brave one.
Your courage lights the way for others still trapped in their darkness.

With fierce respect, boundless love, and unshaken solidarity,
The Writer Who Sees You

Chapter 18: Dear Women Breaking Traditions

Dear Women Breaking Traditions,

This letter is for you; the women who dared to question the rules written long before you were born. The ones who stood at the crossroads of *"what has always been"* and *"what could be,"* and chose the harder, lonelier path because you knew your soul wasn't made for cages.

I see you.

I see the defiance in your eyes when someone tells you *"this isn't how it's done."* I see the quiet rebellion in your choices; whether it's refusing an arranged marriage, pursuing a career when no one else in your family did, choosing not to have children, living alone, speaking up in rooms where women were taught to stay silent, or simply dressing the way you please in a world that loves to police your body.

You've carried the weight of expectations your entire life. You've heard the whispers, felt the stares, and shouldered the guilt others tried to place on you. You've sacrificed relationships, comfort, and sometimes even your safety just to live on your own terms.

Some of you left homes that didn't understand you.
Some of you stayed and fought quietly.
Some of you carved out new spaces in old places, building a life that fit the shape of your spirit, not the mold of tradition.

I want to thank you; for your courage, for your stubborn hope, for enduring the loneliness that often walks beside those who refuse to settle. You've taught generations of girls watching from the sidelines that it's okay to say no, to dream differently, to want more.

Because of you, old chains are breaking.
Because of you, new stories are being written.

Because of you, the world is slowly becoming a place where women are allowed to choose.

You are not rebellious.
You are not selfish.
You are not ungrateful.

You are a pioneer. A torchbearer. A woman who decided to live by the truth in her heart, even when it cost her everything.

And for that; you are deeply loved, respected, and remembered.

With fierce admiration and unwavering solidarity,
The Writer Who Sees You

Chapter 19: Dear Women Dreamers

Dear Women Dreamers,

This letter is for you; the women whose hearts are stitched together with hopes bigger than their circumstances. The ones who stay awake at night imagining lives they've been told they'll never have, who dare to believe in a future that no one else around them can see.

I see you.

I see the spark in your eyes when you speak of the things you long for; the book you want to write, the places you want to travel, the business you dream of starting, the songs you hum in secret. I see the way your chest raises when you picture a life unbound by what people expect from you.

You've carried your dreams in a world that often tells women to be content, to be quiet, to settle. You've faced questions like *"What will people say?"* and *"Is this even possible for someone like you?"* You've sacrificed security, approval, and sometimes relationships to chase something that felt real only to you.

Some of you are chasing careers your families don't understand.
Some of you are dreaming of love that looks different than what tradition says it should.
Some of you are dreaming for the daughters you hope to have one day, or for the little girl you once were.

And though the path hasn't been easy; you've held on. Through rejection, through failures, through days when doubt screamed louder than hope, you've kept a little flame burning inside your chest.

I want to thank you; for believing in yourself when no one else did. For teaching other women that their ambitions don't need to be dimmed to make others comfortable. For dreaming not only for yourself but for the generations of women who were never allowed to.

Your dreams matter.
Your voice matters.
And even if the world takes its time catching up to you; don't stop.

Because the women who dream are the ones who shape new futures. And one day, the world will be better because you refused to let yours die.

With love, faith, and unending encouragement,
The Writer Who Sees You

Chapter 20: Dear Women Who Care for Others

Dear Women Who Care for Others,

This letter is for you; the women whose hearts naturally reach out, whose hands instinctively hold, and whose lives are built around lifting others, often without expecting anything in return.

I see you.

I see the quiet sacrifices you make every day; the meals you prepare for your family before thinking of yourself, the phone calls you answer late at night, the burdens you silently carry on behalf of those you love. I see the tenderness in the way you tend to the sick, comfort the broken, and hold space for those who are falling apart.

You've become the anchor in your homes, your friendships, your workplaces.
You check in on people who never think to ask how you're doing. You remember birthdays, favorite meals, and the weight of other people's sadness. You notice the unspoken, step in where you're needed, and carry the invisible weight of being *the strong one.*

And though it might feel thankless at times; I want to thank you. For the endless cups of tea made for weary hearts. For the tears you've wiped from faces not your own. For showing up when it was inconvenient, uncomfortable, or unnoticed.
For carrying others while quietly tending to your own wounds.

You've sacrificed your time, your energy, and sometimes your dreams to be what others needed. And though the world may overlook the beauty of your compassion, I want to remind you that what you do matters more than you know.

You are the heartbeats of your families, the soul of your friendships, and the light in spaces that would be dim without you.

But dear woman, don't forget to care for yourself too.
Your heart deserves rest.
Your hands deserve to be held.
Your dreams deserve to be honored.

You are not selfish for needing what you so freely give.

So thank you; for your love, your patience, your kindness, and your unbreakable spirit. The world is softer, warmer, and better because of women like you.

With gentle gratitude and heartfelt love,
The Writer Who Sees You

Chapter 21: Dear Forgotten Women

Dear Forgotten Women,

This letter is for you; the women whose names have been lost in the noise, whose faces the world looks past, whose stories remain untold. You are the ones society forgets to mention, the ones left behind in conversations about strength and beauty and worth.

I see you.

I see the women growing old alone, sitting by windows waiting for visitors who don't come. I see the widows, the unmarried women, the women abandoned by those they gave their hearts to. I see the women in the shadows, working behind the scenes, cleaning homes, nursing the sick, raising children that aren't their own; never praised, never remembered.

I see the women whose dreams were shelved because no one asked what they wanted. The women who gave up everything for others and were left with empty rooms and silent phones. I see the women society uses and discards when they no longer fit its idea of youth, beauty, or usefulness.

You've made sacrifices that no one noticed.
You've endured loneliness that would crush others.
You've watched people walk away without a backward glance.
And still; you rise, quietly, every day.

I want to thank you; for your unseen strength. For your quiet courage in living a life without applause. For the kindness you give without expectation, for the wisdom you hold, for the invisible footprints you've left on hearts you may never know you touched.

You matter.
Even if no one tells you.

Even if the world forgets your name.
Even if the room falls silent when you enter.

You matter because you existed. Because you loved. Because you tried.

Your story deserves to be told, your sacrifices deserve to be honored, and your spirit deserves to be celebrated.

So today, I remember you.
I write for you.
And I thank you; for everything you've done, for everything you are.

With quiet reverence, deep love, and eternal remembrance,
The Writer Who Sees You

Chapter 22: Dear Every Woman Who Chose Herself

Dear Every Woman Who Chose Herself,

This letter is for you; the woman who, after years of being everything for everyone else, finally turned inward and whispered, *"I choose me."*

I see you.

I see the battles you fought inside yourself before you made that choice. I see the nights you lay awake, questioning whether you were selfish for wanting more. I see the years you spent putting others before your dreams, your peace, your joy; and the moment you realized that you could no longer keep breaking yourself to keep everyone else whole.

You walked away from relationships, expectations, traditions, and obligations that no longer honored your soul. You stopped apologizing for your ambitions, your boundaries, and your voice. You learned to say *no* without guilt and *yes* without seeking permission.

It wasn't easy.
You lost people. You were judged. You heard the whispers.
You carried the heavy weight of disappointing those who benefitted from your silence and sacrifice. But you chose yourself anyway.

I want to thank you; for the courage it took to stand alone. For the tears you cried when no one knew how hard it was to unlearn a lifetime of pleasing. For choosing peace over approval, happiness over appearance, and truth over comfort.

You are not selfish.
You are not heartless.
You are not rebellious.

You are a woman reclaiming her life. A woman teaching others that it's never too late to begin again, to rewrite the story, to build a home inside yourself that feels like freedom.

And because you chose yourself, you'll inspire other women to believe they can too.

So here's to you; the woman who said, *"I matter."*
Your bravery is the quiet revolution this world so desperately needs.

With deep pride, love, and unshaken solidarity,
The Writer Who Sees You

Chapter 23: Dear Women Who Support Other Women

Dear Women Who Support Other Women,

This letter is for you; the ones who refuse to see other women as competition, who knows that the world is kinder, safer, and stronger when we hold each other up.

I see you.

I see the way you clap the loudest when a woman rises, how you defend her when she's not in the room, how you reach out when you sense another woman breaking under the weight of expectations. I see the way you celebrate not just your own victories, but hers too.

You've carried your own pain, and instead of letting it harden you, you chose to turn it into understanding. You became the voice that says *"I've been there"* and *"You're not alone."* You became the friend who listens without judging, the stranger who offers encouragement, the sister who reminds another woman of her worth.

You've sacrificed your time, your energy, sometimes your peace, to be a steady hand for someone else. You've shared opportunities, opened doors, and reminded other women that they deserve to take up space, to speak, to lead, to dream.

And in a world that often teaches women to tear each other down, you chose differently.
You chose solidarity over rivalry.
Empathy over envy.
Kindness over cruelty.

I want to thank you; for being a soft place to land in a harsh world. For teaching other women that there's room for all of us. For proving that when women stand together, we are unstoppable.

Your support is a quiet rebellion.
Your kindness is a light in the dark.
Your courage to lift others is a legacy.

And though you may never get the recognition you deserve, know this: you are making this world better, one woman at a time.

With fierce gratitude, endless admiration, and sisterhood in every word,
The Writer Who Sees You

Chapter 24: Dear Women Who Hurt Men

Dear Women Who Hurt Men,

This letter is for you; the ones who think betrayal is clever, who take the care given by a man and treat it as nothing, who forget the love and sacrifices that once held your world together.

I see you.

I see the way you dismiss his efforts, how you take his late-night calls, his quiet worries, his hard work, and fold them into something ordinary, as if they were never extraordinary acts of love. I see the way you forget the days he stood beside you when no one else did, how you erase the sacrifices he made so you could dream a little bigger, sleep a little easier, smile a little more.

I see the way you use his trust as a game piece, moving it around to win your own battles, without realizing the cost. I see how you take his vulnerability; those rare moments when he lets the armor drop; and turn them into weapons. I see how you walk away, convinced you've outsmarted him, when in truth, and you've only taught him to guard his heart from love itself.

Men are not unshakable mountains. They bleed quietly. They break silently. And when they are hurt by the woman they trusted most, something deep inside them changes; sometimes forever. They stop believing in love the way they once did. They carry an invisible heaviness into every new beginning.

If you've done this because you thought his feelings didn't matter, you were wrong. If you've done this thinking you were clever, you've mistaken cruelty for intelligence. And if you've done this without care, remember; love is not limitless when met with neglect.

This is not to curse you, but to wake you. To remind you that every act of betrayal leaves a scar, every dismissal leaves a hollow space where trust used to live. You can choose differently. You can see the care he gives as the gift it is. You can honor the sacrifices made for you instead of erasing them.

Because the truth is, when love is met with gratitude, it grows. When care is recognized, it strengthens bonds. And when loyalty is returned, both hearts rise together.

For the men you've hurt; the ones who gave more than they got; I hope one day you understand the weight of what was lost. And I hope you find the courage to be better, not just for them, but for yourself.

With truth, hope, and the belief that we can all do better,
The Writer Who Sees You Too

Chapter 25: Dear Every Woman

Dear Every Woman,

This final letter is for you; wherever you are, whatever you've endured, whoever you've become.

I see you.

I see the courage it takes just to wake up some days. I see the battles you fight behind your smile, the dreams you carry in your heart, the fears you never speak aloud. I see the way you love, the way you hurt, the way you rise; even after being broken.

You are the little girl learning how to navigate a world that tries to shrink her spirit.
You are the teenager wrestling with her reflection and the weight of other people's expectations.
You are the sister holding a family together in silence.
You are the housewife making a home out of nothing but sacrifice and heart.
You are the mother loving beyond exhaustion.
You are the widow learning how to breathe alone.
You are the unmarried woman forging her own path.
You are the working woman juggling dreams and duties.
You are the divorced woman rebuilding from the ashes.
You are the survivor of heartbreak, of loss, of abuse.
You are the dreamer, the rebel, the nurturer, the healer, the fighter.

And in all your forms; you matter.

This world owes you gratitude it can never repay. For the silent sacrifices, the courage unseen, the tenderness you give even when no one returns it. You are the stories whispered through generations. The blood memory of every woman who came before you. The fierce protector of every woman who will come after.

I want to thank you; not just for what you do, but for who you are.
For your warmth, your wisdom, your resilience.
For continuing to believe in light, even after walking through darkness.
For every time you chose to get up, to keep going, to hold on to yourself when the world tried to make you forget who you were.

You are not alone.
You are not invisible.
You are not forgotten.

This book was written for you.
To honor your story.
To thank you for existing.
To remind you that you are worthy, not because of what you give others, but because of who you are.

You; in all your flawed, brilliant, beautiful, complicated humanity; are enough.

With endless love, respect, and eternal solidarity,
The Writer Who Sees You

Chapter 26: Final Message: From the Writer Who Sees You

To every woman who held this book in her hands, who paused her day to read these words, who saw herself; or someone she loves; in these pages, this message is for you.

When I first began writing these letters, I didn't know all the faces they would reach. I didn't know if anyone would pause long enough to hear them. But I wrote them anyway, because every woman deserves to be seen, heard, and honored. Not just for what she gives to the world, but for who she is when no one's watching.

This book is more than a collection of letters; it's a tribute. A quiet, tender rebellion against a world that often moves too fast to notice the struggles, sacrifices, and silent strengths of women in every stage of life. It's a mirror for the little girl inside you, for the sister beside you, for the mother you miss, for the friend you lean on, and for the woman you're still becoming.

To the women who sacrificed without acknowledgment,
To the ones who loved without conditions,
To those who broke, healed, and rose again; even when no one cheered for them,
To the ones who chose themselves for the first time, and the ones still gathering the courage to,

I wrote for you.

I hope these words reminded you of your worth. I hope they felt like a hand in yours on the loneliest days. I hope you felt seen, not just in the victories but in the mess, the exhaustion, the compromises, and the quiet bravery it takes to live a woman's life.

And if no one has told you lately; thank you.
For existing.
For continuing.
For hoping.
For making the world gentler, stronger, and more beautiful by simply being here.

This is not goodbye.
These words will be waiting for you whenever you need them again.
And wherever you go next in life, may you remember that you belong, that your story matters. And that someone out here is forever proud of you.

With all my heart,
Muzzafar Badder

---

9 789334 298352

Printed at Repro India Ltd.